The Moving Waters

Mary Jane Ryals

Mary Jane Ryals

1-23-09

Kitsune Books

Quality books for eclectic readers

The Moving Waters

Kitsune Books
P.O. Box 1154
Crawfordville, FL 32326-1154

www.kitsunebooks.com
contact@kitsunebooks.com

Printed in USA
First printing in 2008

ISBN-13: 978-0-9792700-4-8
ISBN-10: 0-9792700-4-9

Library of Congress Control Number: 2007935181

Cover design: Lynne Knight
Front and back cover photos: Mary Jane Ryals
Author portrait: Inga Finch

First edition

The Moving Waters

Don't you realize that the sea is the home of water? All water is off on a journey unless it's in the sea, and it's homesick, and bound to make its way home someday.

~Zora Neale Hurston

Pardon me, if when I want
to tell the story of my life
it's the land I talk about.
This is the land.
It grows in your blood
and you grow.
If it dies in your blood
you die out.

~Pablo Neruda

Acknowledgements

Grateful acknowledgement is due to the following periodicals, in which poems appearing in this volume were originally published:

Music in Arabic...*Phoebe*, chapbook*
The Wash: *Lavandería con sus Manos*...*Calyx*
Shoes in Spain...*13ᵗʰ Moon*
En la Noche...*13ᵗʰ Moon*
Postcard to Michael from Spain...*Snake Nation Review*
Daughter, I Am Taking You to Belfast...*Analecta XIX* contest winner
Hanoi Pantoum...chapbook*
Ode to Turquoise in Vietnam...chapbook*
To My Daughter at 12 in Vietnam...chapbook*
To My Children on Father's Day...*Tallahassee Democrat*
Planetarium Field Trip...*Tallahassee Democrat*
Blessings...*Cimarron Review*
Daughter,...*Spinning Jenny*
Horse Grace...*Cincinnati Poets Collective*
Remembering Pop...*Snug*
Ode to Driving at Night...chapbook*
Charleston Garden...*Beacon Street Review*
September Wind, 2005...chapbook*
The Kiss...*Poetry Motel*
In the Motel Room...*The New Delta Review*
The Sestina of an Unmarried Mother...*Cimarron Review, 13 Ways of Looking at a Poem*

Arrival, Oaxaca, Mexico...*juked*
Majorelle Gardens...chapbook*
Gulbenkien Museum and La Chata...*Louisiana Literature*
The Butcher Knows...*poetrysouth*
Columbus' Discovery of America...*Simon Daro Davidowicz poetry
   contest winner, Carolyn Forche, judge*
A Word to Sylvia Plath...*Apalachee Quarterly*
How to Make a Baby...*Mothering Magazine*
They Showed Me the Creek...*The Texas Review*
What I'll Tell the Martians....*CaKe*

*Chapbook—winner, Florida Chapbook Contest, 2006 for *Music
in Arabic*

For financial support and for the setting in which to write with
solitude or stimulation, thanks to The Hambidge Center, Atlantic
Center for the Arts, the Florida State University Management
Department, the Florida Arts Council, the National Endowment
for the Humanities and the Rockefeller Foundation, and the FSU
International Programs in Spain.

Special thanks to "The Javas": Donna Decker, Lynne Knight, Laura
Newton, and Melanie Rawls for their sustenance. Bruce Lamont,
many thanks for the ear, understanding and time. To Anne Petty,
thanks for believing.

Thank also to Lynn Holschuh of Kitsune Books for copyediting.

for my husband, Michael Trammell

CONTENTS

v. field that cups a pond

vi. swim uncaught

vii. the blood-black swamp

viii. tide at its neap extremes

ix. skimming like lost history

PROLOGUE

Water Women
—for Pam Ball

My ancestors, women
of Mediterranean Seas,
Appalachian streams, Irish Oceans,
emptied themselves into
Virginia and the Carolinas carrying bags
of baby fishes and luck:
heirlooms from weddings and funerals.
Their skeletons
carved from shark bones, their breath
the scent of salty air and fins;
they turned men solid in their embrace.
their children turned mineral
or evaporated,
the element of luck.

This heirloom,
their baby fish skeletons in my belly, passed
from mother to daughter to granddaughter,
generations of water women in my belly.
They crash their waves at my beach every year,
their voices hushing and constant.

No, they won't let me out of the water,
and I promise myself
even if I'm the last water woman,
that I'll ride the waves into summer
on their bellies.

i. the wash by hand:

Lavandería con sus Manos

The Wash: *Lavandería con sus Manos*

Just back to Spain from Prague with a sore throat
aching your ears, you kneel on the marble floor
regarding the mass of clothes in the tub.
You look closer, and it's Picasso's stratosphere

of color and form, and there appears a mermaid eye
and her hand, holding an open box of *jabón
natural con perfumera,* the fragrance
of lavender, rosemary and lemon. Your hands

on your own clothing, cotton, sturdy and heavy
as dolphins, rayon lighter than starfish, silk stiff
as sea grass in your hand, but dries even as you twist
water out. Like saying a rosary, you attend

to each holy garment, knowing what needs care: this
orange t-shirt under the arms the day you charged
up the mountain, the front of the white dress shirt
where you spilt chocolate in the Italian restaurant,

those jeans you smeared lipstick onto as you admired
St. Vitus Cathedral, the tallest you've seen.
You rinse them in the sea of Mediterranean
water in the sink, then toss open the balcony

door to ocean air, morning breeze on your skin.
You lay out clothes as if offering water to the sun.
Below, the fat earth and its daily dramas: people
walking to work, the tram emptying, filling, birds

chirping, the mountains behind, and you want to sing

and wash clothes by hand forever when your ears throb
in pain. You slip slop back into the room and curl
under cover for a long *siesta* with the *Virgen*

de Remedio, Señora of Healing. The sun
has already pulled wet sorrow from the sheets,
and you breathe, thanking the spirits of
your grandmothers for fresh laundry.

Shoes in Spain
—with a nod to Garcia Lorca

I.

When first lady Imelda Marcos got busted
for owning 1,220 pairs of shoes

and her people starved, half the women
in the world squirmed. Shoes.

After all, wouldn't most of us dream
of owning Renaissance courtiers' clothing,

as many *zapatos* as possible?
One pair to cry in, one to shout in,

one pair for singing, one to play and dance in.
"I am not rational about shoes,"

says my Spanish friend Belen.
"Belen could swim in shoes,"

her husband jokes. She may as well have
raised Lazarus from the dead for the miracle

she accomplishes, luring her American students
into falling in love with Spanish. And her zapatos?

The students adore her sky-colored,
star shimmering sandals, her flamenco red shoes,

and her Degas inspired ballet slippers.
They are the clanging of bells in the morning tower.

II.

I sacrificed a week's grocery money before I left the U.S.,
torn between ugly function and ugly dollars for Mephisto shoes.

Even the name should warn you—wasn't it Mephisto
who betrayed everyone in Nazi Germany? "Your shoes

give you away as an American—sandals and white socks,"
BJ said when I arrived. So Belen led me to the shoe stores,

as if taking a camel with no hump to water. She coaxed me into
the turquoise-beaded, amber-studded sandals, arabesque

in design, that I now wear. Are not shoes
a manifestation of style over function?

A sign we needn't wrap feet in barbarian
animal hide, but that we've learned how

 to live? Art over function?
Or am I just a conspicuous consumer?

Or do I just admire a woman like Friday Kahlo
who knew how to dress, make art, and wear good shoes?

III.

Which brings up another question of the divided self:
Take my South Carolina grandmother, Nana,

who shucked the farm shoes for college,
moved to then-exotic, palm-lined Florida beaches,

met a man with a sharp crease in his suit pants,
lace-up leather shoes, signs he was moving up in the world,

and she began to collect high heel pumps.
T-bar jazz age flappers from the Roaring 20s,

two-tones from the 40s, satin studded pumps in the 50s,
the first century Americans had luxury and fashion.

A few years earlier Picasso had broken free,
painting a frond of stars called *Les Demoiselles d'Avignon*,

and later Nana adored Salvador Dali jewelry.
Still, after she designed and built

her Spanish-style house in Orlando,
full of Venetian glass, so far from the farm,

she kept chickens in the back yard.
My mother told me that on Saturdays,

Nana would brandish a knife like a conquistador,
chase a hen around, catch it by the neck and chop

off its head, planning for Sunday's dinner. My mother,
in macabre fascination, gave me the lurid detail.

What shoes did my grandmother wear as she
spilled blood? Hearts of silk,

dark caves with windows of gold,
warm lily regions of white sorrow?

Maybe we need a pair of shoes for killing,
too, though I am still stuck with Imelda,

cold of heart and baroque with shoes,
a sin. Pardon my irreverence here,

but even my Presbyterian upbringing
had some decent thoughts—give to the poor,

show compassion for others,
work for peace not war, and

never did I hear that I should
not buy *zapatos bonitos*, which

if you ask me, sounds like Spanish
for *café con leche,* chocolate and kisses

for nights of scarlet and thirsting mouths,
for nights of a pounding, sanguine dance.

Praise for Spanish Women

—Have you committed a fashion slipup? **Then you need this book!** *Glamour's Big Book of Dos and Don'ts*

Praise the seventy-year-old senora, still
dyeing her hair in an up-do like Liz Taylor
in *Black Beauty* as she turned twelve.

Praise the woman with a gem-studded
Mickey Mouse shirt so tight her bra lines
and back fat are revealed, and she does

not despair. Praise *l'abuela* in black-
and-white fashion skirt, her belly a swell of
memory—*See what I brought this world?*

Praise what's in front of us if we would let it be:
meatball arms and spaghetti straps in beach heat.
Praise the blue sky that still holds itself up, and

summer nights that swim. Praise *las mujeres*
who don skirts that flower into fiestas, and step
into dark hose like fishermen's nets that somehow

match white sandals. Praise their *maridos* parading
next to them on the *Ponte de Fusta* bridge, offering
elbows as bows for their wives' elegant arrows.

Praise the lady with orange *zapatos* that match
nothing she wears, and who anchors her palm
under her stooped mother's arm, guiding

her across busy *Calle Cronista Rivelles*, as though
every ounce of her mother was a recovered chest of coins.
Praise this wild runway, this don't give a damn chic.

Picasso's *La Chata,* the Pug Nose Lady

Whatever I expect here while sitting outside
the museum on a Roman stone does not matter

yet, since the sliver of sun slanting through
the alleyway on an afternoon Medieval street is

ecstasy anyway. But Picasso never had me dreaming
on a train; Cubism leaves me wanting Spanish

apples on a tree, or cherries, oranges, as do
his obsessive sketches of naked women

posing to show their "privacy," what my daughter
called *it* as a baby. Once inside the museum,

a Renaissance building, I see his early period paintings,
lines of mountains, landscapes, portraits,

then roomfuls of grayish impressionism, imitation
Goya, all common as socks. In Paris, the blue period—

painting the outcasts, each with *un azul* background, sad,
and—funny! La Chata, a cigarette drooping from

her mouth, her scowl showing wrinkled disgust
with this world, yet she hangs on with high

teased hair dyed blue-black. She is a combination
of my small-town great aunts and gargoyles

on a Spanish castle. Of course! How the horrible
becomes humorous in a world of tragedy, like Picasso's

20th century Europe, or my many divorced aunts,
hell-raising, cussing and smoking, children car

wrecked or killed by AIDS in this changing world.
I feel *un pocito* like my great aunts, a sore throat

bruising my throat for weeks now in Europe. Some
day, I will look like *La Chata* with deep wrinkles,

her slump, the bouffant. Odd—this makes me laugh.
I shuffle on, through Picasso's cartoons of sex acts,

where American girls in the museum say *Ew*
to the oral sex, and older French women roll

their eyes. On to the Cubist period where Picasso
was pushing yet again. To the last phase

of his life, the ceramics, elaborate and wild plates,
one with a cat at the bottom, a clay fish offered

on top, as if challenging the viewer to lunge at
the cat over food. Suddenly I see Picasso chuckling

in the dark—clay on his hands, nose, and his striped
shirt—laughing like we all do growing older.

I follow sweet sweaty, field-tripping Spanish high
schoolers outside. The day lingers long, the way

they do in Spanish summers, my poster of
La Chata, a gift from Picasso for helping

us look in the mirror and laugh like teens. Hard.

The Butcher, Valencia, Spain after 9-11

How is this world? Does the butcher know?
At *el Carnicaria Lahoz* across my street,
she moves with the panache of the tilde.
She asks me, the American, what I want.

I point to dead chickens, plucked, heads
and claws on. I say *El pollo* in broken
Español, say *medio,* wondering how bruised
our world is. I slash hand-across-neck, my face

a wince, to indicate what I have never seen
and do not want. She nods, smiles, sees
the troubled look. *Pero, no,* I say, slicing
a finger across my neck. She guffaws,

nodding, takes the chicken as if a flower stem
by the neck and places it bouquetlike on the table,
picks up the cleaver. In one sweet motion
the head plunges into the garbage. What does

the butcher know? Now it's a game of show
and don't tell. She points to the claws, her eyebrows
raised in a mock shock, teasing at this game, smiles
and says, *¿Y las patas?* Also, I say, *También.*

She gives me a decided nod, and off go the feet.
My Japanese friend says about the Spanish:
*Never have I seen people put so much effort
into having a good time!* The butcher knows.

Only decades from civil war and no bread,
from brother killing brother, from no toothbrushes,

no TV's or music, Spaniards know there's only
laughter. I'm tired of my country's certainty,

our bombs, our revenge, even packaged chicken—
an idea wrapped in plastic, already stamped and
priced. Oh, the butcher knows. By this can we live,
crying for the chickens, laughing at ourselves?

En la Noche del Apartamento en el decimosexto piso

La luna flota sobre la ciudad.
¡Como ella adula las luces de abajo!
Las luces humanas y tontas,
Los colores de un mango, del cielo,
El mar, emiten, imitan.
La luna canta la melodia paciente
Del viento de los gitanos.

Translation:

In the Night from the 16th floor Apartment

The moon floats over the city.
How it flatters the lights below!
Silly human lights,
Colors of a mango, the sky,
The sea. They emit, they imitate.
The moon sings the patient
Wind melody of the gypsies.

Finding Moses in Madrid

i. Brightness

This poem begins with tears in front of a painting.
Moisés de la Aguas, "The Finding of Moses,"

but that's almost past the story where I'm stupid
as Venus clinging to Adonis in another painting

also hanging in *El Prado Museo*. Damn her—a goddess,
after all—wanting a guy who'd rather hunt than hang

with her, the way it goes with my husband right now
while we're teaching three classes each, stumbling

in *Español*, not liking change, but trying. Absurd
to ponder his misplacing me in *Museo Reina Sofía*

where Picasso's *Guernica* stretches across rooms,
where he was absorbed in Miro's personal mythology.

So why boo-hoo? But this isn't why I'm crying.
My son at eighteen blew up when we waked him too early,

today howled because we woke him too late, my ten-year-old
daughter swiped our friends' clock, but refuses to play

John Hinkley, plead guilty and be done with it.
And the four of us are lodging in an itty bitty room,

though a shabby genteel inn, The Hotel Paris, 95 F outside,
 an iffy crib a.c., and with cars, millions of walkers,

the parched statues, the brightness, I feel certain
if God decides we blow it on earth, don't make

the cut into heaven, then we will end up
walking this *Plaza del Sol* in July

for eternity where Dylan was robbed
this morning of a hundred Euros.

ii. Darkness

I will end up in the stench of congealed blood,
in a hog's ear-muzzle, or a rat nose-to-nose with me

in the darkness of Bosch's *Worldly Delights*,
only now I'd be grateful, since *les luz* makes

this Pavlov dog think cool. And have you noticed
that dogs will eat anything? You can see my mind

has wavered astray...which reminds me
of Goya's painting where Saturn is eating his children

to keep the prophecy from coming true—
that one of his kids would kill him.

The monstrous picture hung in Goya's room
where he dined with wife and kids...and it came to nothing,

not the painting, but the consumption of *el niños*,
because Saturn's wife hid the kid who grew up

to kill his father. Dreary. But back from this digression.
On the hot walk to the museum, a building is spray-painted,

Yankis Go Home, and Fuck the US, which I understand, but...
then I get directions to a bank just past *The Hotel Grande,*

Hemingway's haunt so chi-chi, so Americanized now
that he could never afford it, when on the street

a Spanish woman stops me, says in broken urgent English
that I'm not from here, and that I must curl my fingers

into my palms, thus avoiding picking up "bad things"
on the street. This disturbs me, because I think

she sounds sane. After I'm nearly flattened
on *Avenida Prado* by a Smart Car, I stand

outside the museum an hour to see Titian,
only to stand another hour inside.

I wander to another painting. O! The tedium of travel
that no one writes about! (No wonder—it's boring).

iii. Float away forever

Back to Moses—this painting's *funny*—
by Venetian Gentileschi, and there circle eight

women (seven slaves) around a baby boy.
So the princess in her low-cut Renaissance gown

points at the baby and stares—her expression!—
in disdain at his male body parts. I am chuckling

when the audioguide in BritishEnglish tells the story

of how Egyptians heard gossip of newborn Hebrew

who would lead said slaves from bondage.
Imagine mothers hearing the decree that their boy babies

would die! Then for a mother to put her newborn
in a basket as his mother did, and lay him atop a river,

watch him float away *siempre*, forever...
but no. As the story of fate goes, Egyptian princess

finds him, likes him (seemingly despite body parts,
ethnicity, class, and etcetera), and asks one of her slave maids

to nurse him. *Voilà*—enter kneeling maid of painting,
frozen in time—true mother to the child, selected at random

to suckle her own child, the one she left to luck at the river.
She can never reveal she *is* the real mother, but it's not a

perfect life,
is it?

iv. Fate

And I am snuffling in a museum, because I have children
I hope I can keep, a husband who will lie down next to me,

with a look say, I will do what it takes to keep this, and I am,
after all, sleeping in a. c. at the Times Square of Spain,

lounging in a lobby with a chandelier, plush Elizabethan chairs,
copies of Velazquez from *El Prado*, a terrace of green and black

tiles, and I do not want to move, but to absorb
this moment that Gentileschi understood,

not of Fate and of eating your children, but the story
of how sometimes Fate delivers you

to the left hand of Bosch's triptych, to the god with a pink robe,
Adam and Eve in an orange grove, to the second chance,

almost to heaven where your children laugh and jump on beds
when you get back from *El Prado*, and angels float down

like bed feathers from coral fountains

                              into your life.

Midnight on the *Plaza de la Virgen*

Each of seven goddesses leans on one hip
After pouring jugs of water from the fountain
all day, while lazy Neptune lounges.

To the left stands the *Catedral,* where
a withered arm of third century martyr
San Vincent is encased, and where two

Goya paintings hang. And here is *la vida,*
kids with dyed hair and piercings, knights
in training, try tricks on skateboards down

Basilica stairs. To the right, parents,
grandparents, and children all out, having
forgotten the rules of midnight, dipping

into a strawberry *helado*, or drinking
a *cerveza,* a *café con leche*, chatting.
A few sunburned British or German

tourists still wander the plaza beyond
the summer day. Doves hawk for bread,
gypsies have retired to burnt out buildings

by the beach. *La luna* glams silver as
earrings Latinos sell in *el Carmen*
down the *calle*. In the day, Brazilian

street dancers fumed like the petrol from
traffic, and nearly broke into three fistfights
under sun's furnace. The gypsies hounded me

for more as I ate *la foccacia atún*; just now
I think of Picasso's *Guernica,* which indicts
Franco's fascist rule, portraying people broken

by the horrible daylight of bombs. But this
constant celebration—night conquering day
with slow patience, like that of *La Virgen*

de los Desamparados, the Virgin of the Abandoned,
Helpless and Poor, *La Patroness* of Valencia.
Our first night here, we sat watching a soccer game

of 12-year-old boys—barely a new century,
before our twin towers went to dust. Such pleasure
that night, despite. *They will never believe this*

back home, I said. *People playing downtown at*
midnight. Back home, I brace for what might jump
out around the next corner. We all come from

violence, yet here, I wait like a teenager in love for
what meets me in an alley, dark chocolate, red wine
of *Rioja,* mosaic tiles, medieval streets, Islamic columns,

Roman baths, Visigoth well, Gothic silk houses, a Baroque
façade. The world keeps insisting itself into being.

Ring Around the Plaza of Justice Rosies
—Valencia, Spain

John, Susan and daughter Sophia step off
the bus into the Plaza de Ayuntamiento, and
cathedral bells ring half past seven, a fountain

bursts forth in tambourine song, and buses play
base drum. In tune with the world, two-year-old
Sophia sings, *Ring around the rosies*, in la plaza

full of flores for sale, and where later they will watch
young lovers serenade with sweet lips and limbs.
Sophia pulls her mother towards my husband Michael,

and she grabs his hand. John takes Susan's,
and they all circle slowly, *A pocket full of posies,*
they all sing, cheerful as kitchen-white counters,

and en Inglés in España. Sophia knows what's deep
under this plaza, ghosts of the Arab city, knows what's
in the cathedral under glass—the withered, blackened

arm of Saint Vincent, only two squares away. *Ashes,*
the ring of them chants, and a car honks in high B.
The world spins around them, white lilies scenting

up the air, *Ashes,* the moon silverful this evening over
the frieze of judges in their graves 200 years now.
The ring of friends drops like the discarded onto

dusty stone, caught in Sophia's unexpected gift of
Sing-and-Dance-Now,
                              We all fall down.

Sweating in Spain, May 2003

I'm elbowing into the holiday crowd
at the *Traslado de Virgen de los Desamparados*,
saint of beggars, orphans, maybe thieves, and

somehow remembering Michael and me leaving
that party to get beer and Mother's Day cards,
but mainly the philosophers were yelling at each other

about naturalism and I forget what. Michael sneered
over Valentines Day, muttering, *Marketing*,
and how sad it made me. *Can't you spend a buck on*

your ole mama? I thought, but didn't say. How
uncool, reminding this younger man I was single mother
to a son. And in fact, it *is* Mother's Day today and

my children in the States reminded me with an amethyst
to stave off homesickness. I have none. I'm huddled
with dark-haired, small people like me while the procession

parades this circle by Turia's fountain—Celtic cross,
ancient priests with pompoms, while balconied girls in gowns
toss rose petals, the crowd chanting, *Guapa Mare*, Beautiful

Mother! Church bells clang, and suddenly, we are all pushed
nearly *into* the fountain. Astonishing, *muy hombres* holding up
the virgin and child on gold pedestal. Some grope, kiss

her feet, others fend off the crowd. We sweat, our hair wet,
raining faces, we pant like dogs, and I am reminded when
that same Michael two years later chased down my car—

I was pregnant, angry, had left him home—yet, he raced down
the street on foot after the car, me braking at the Stop.
He lept into air and slam! Sprawled onto the trunk

of the car like Spiderman, only with more gravity. I got out
to find him sitting on the bumper, sweating, panting, working
hard to save our love. Dear readers, how men work so hard

for us. And how mothers' bodies work to get us here;
 and how hard we all work to get into this world.

Gifts from across the Water
—for Laura, Lynne, Donna, and Melanie

Every year, I bring
something back for you—

Arabic brass earrings shaped
like teardrops, lantern

and desert; one year silver
in optical art exuberance

of Spain—the red beads,
a *duende* in blood and dance.

Last year, the glass hearts
from Italy streaked with colors

of sky, gild, black marble.
But these do not touch

the deep wide stones long
as a leg, foundations built

by Romans almost two
thousand years ago.

That feel of earth—who else
has left dust on such stones?

A medieval goat herder?
An Arabic woman singing her way

to the bread baker? A fisherman

smelling of sardines and liking it?

A young girl holding her belly?
In this poem, I bring you

fresh pesto home,
calamari just off the boat,

market strawberries dusty with dirt.
Nuances of Spanish olive skin

and the sculpted beauty Spaniards
flaunt without flaunting,

the outside cafes where
time sits and has a smoke,

and does not treadmill
but swings its way through the city

window shopping for words,
not stuff that replaces the living.

Leaving Spain
—for Wendy Bishop (1953 - 2003)

I want a hotel, dark and linen
And the room to fill with aquamarine floor

I want Moorish palms to appear on walls
And my hair to catch African winds at night

If the French lavender and the Arabic cubed candy infused
With rosewater could only chase me home

I want the moon shining a white rabbit above
And the sheer Indian tunics drowning out our suits

I fear nights back home smothered in tires and
Guns and my coughing off days and dollars

I fight against graphs and charts of war
And invite us to touch the bones of suffering

But Spain, leave me the simple spinach and goat
Cheese sandwiches of Medieval Catalan

But then let me forget your sweet melon.
Do not follow my narrow highway home.

ii. sun sends stars to fountain's water

Music in Arabic

This bar is an orchestra pit full of empty chairs,
and maybe the bus to the plane will leave
me in this posh Moroccan hotel forever.

The staff, three men, *arrajelo,* speak some English,
no women *(al marat)* but me. I ask for *al maa,*
water, and a piece of paper, a pen.

The water chills my throat, and I draw
a flower, push it to the bartender, and he writes
al ward. I say cow, and the three of them puzzle.

I bellow *Mrawooooo,* and we all laugh,
and they nod *al baker* as the bartender writes
from right to left in elegant sweeps and dots.

Here at *El Andalus* in Marrakech, the ceiling fans
keep turning, and I don't ask the word for war, and
they shine bar glasses clear as African sky.

Buses are painted turquoise, and stop signs
are curlicues on red octagons. *Dawg, you ain't never
seen a place like this,* I think of saying to

friends back home as one of the staffers
gobbles like a turkey. We are laughing
so hard tears form, and the bartender

writes *bibi.* Donkeys are the Toyotas
of these streets. Perhaps we will soon need
carrots to run our cars. The *al farah al himar*

of *al hobe* is our *al helm*, I say. We laugh
like school kids at dreaming of the happy
donkey of love. Soft smell of mule ears

makes me want to stay another day, another month.
I will. I will buy carrots from the Medina
and feed every Toyota in the city. I don't know

how to get to the airport. Maybe I can sing
my way on a camel to the ocean and swim
a song on the back of *al hissan*, a horse,

to Europe, because music is *music*
in Arabic.

Writing Checks, 2003

Spain, world at the edge
　　　　of Europe, Morocco and Israel,
　　　　place of palms, sand, desert, mountains,
　　　　and the last bombing;
I now write checks to cover expenses
in Florida but eat up my book of Spanish phrases.

No me siento seguara aqui,
　　　　I don't feel safe here, and
　　　　¿Por qué estás riendo?...Hablo español tan mal?
　　　　Why are you laughing?...Is my Spanish that bad?
I would be afraid if I were you, some say.

Sometimes I want to marry Spain,
　　　　gather *azul y amarillo*
　　　　dishes for the *cocina,*
　　　　build *un casa* from Moorish stone in
　　　　las montañas, dance forever
　　　　on moon-colored sands.

I finish writing checks, 20 of them, paper clip them
as if it were all so easy, and walk outside,
remember the line from Thailand:
　　　　"Life is short, we must move very slowly."

A cardinal starts up, another.
The woods are lime green gilt,
　　　　verde, verdant.

I lie in the hammock;
　　　　why is my daughter
　　　　the only one who does this?

Mockingbirds join in, and
> the scent of pines,
> geese honking,
> a shy sky peeking
> between oak branches.

These woods,
> *selva*, forest,
> *bosque*; jungle—
Spaniard friends say English is a jungle of a language.

I think of *Isle d'Fac*,
> drama of a rock jutting straight up
> out of the turquoise Mediterranean
> pointing to the sky,
> lavender and daisies
> dressing the peak.

Look at the sky—
> It is worth writing checks
> in the clouds
> for all our lives.

Majorelle Gardens

The lacy Islamic doors lure you to the garden,
the walls packed with blue so blue it bears
its own name, *Bleu Majorelle*, Mediterranean blue,
then green of cactus, of sabal palm, of bamboo.

A wagon and donkey clop past the doors
in dust and orange light. Sun sends stars
to fountain's water, water passes them
to us, armfuls of lotus, water lilies, papyrus.

My heart is mad and ready for such musk.
I came to see this, though I didn't know till now.
Past the tangle of monkey puzzle tree
and hot pink bougainvillea, I breathe *bleu*

Majorelle, and stop to watch a man stooped
at work, his Moroccan skin the color that
almonds envy. He scrapes *bleu Majorelle*
from the orange pot with a tool shaped like

Fatima's hand. Slowly, her hand chisels. Time
is intoxicated here, art echo of a thousand years.
My young country knows no words for age and
art. The fragrance of orange tree ripples air.

Tu as de la chance de travailler ici,
I say in French. *You are lucky to work here.*
Tu as de la chance de visiter,
he says. *You are lucky to visit.*

Gulbenkian Museum, Portugal

This time of day, we all want a nap. French
widows discuss their children in baritone

voices. A Portuguese man pores over his
newspaper. The lobby loosens a sudden quiet

like an empty confession booth. We're
surrounded by the lost loot of empires: sleek

Egyptian cats, painted Arabic glass, Greek coins.
Low black chairs take our western weight in clean

lines and comfort cushions. Maybe *The Thinker*
was just napping. The shag carpet feels cat fur beige,

and outside, the heat's reaching 90 degrees.
A cathedral cool hums through the a.c., and

the glass wall looks out onto nuts of palm trees,
hanging in ropes down the trunk, heavy as Mary's

lazy diverted eyes in Italian paintings--perhaps she
was simply caught dozing. Or the *Girl with Fan* falling

still in Pinasso's Spanish impressionism.
Sometimes there's nothing more than this.

Rondini

One swallow does not mean Spring,
        the Italians say, a warning against
                winter's early lifting. Here in summer,

                the Lamborghini of birds, these *rondini,*
                        sleek black bodies, red cheeks, breast
                                showy white as platinum, return,

                        as they do each year, to settle in homes—
                                the same *casa* every year in villages
                                that jostle among Mediterranean cliffs.

                        Monogamous. No wonder
                the Italians watch for their annual
        resurrection, as they thrive winters

                warm in Africa, then wing, freckling
        shadows across teal water, following
lemons, terraces, the best life possible.

Arrival, Oaxaca, Mexico

The courtyard of this Southern Mexico
apartment is shaded by the smiling
boughs of a grapefruit tree that furnishes

home to a pair of birds who politely
shit the floor, and where we wake mornings
to georgic bells that fill the air,

a rooster that *ki-ki-keyrie-ki's* early and
surrounds the city sounds. If words could,
they would transform into perfume of

grapefruit-blossom scent. When did this
happen in my own country, that lounging
requires leaving it? At home, we are all

cars, errands, work. The color here, oh--
bougainvillea petals gang up together
on the wall in hot bouquets of *rojo*, coral *y*

blanco. Flowers weed out fierce while we
aristocrats lounge in our ruining state. This
culture, 2,000 years old, could give a bird's

shit about us. What relief, the pressure off!
The end of day goes violet here, so nearly
blood orange, it makes me want to weep color.

Daughter, I am taking you to Belfast, 1992

Pregnant with you, I train in from Islangmagee,
passing the choppy Irish Sea, places named
Greenisland and Carrickfergus. At Belfast's City Center
people scutter quiet as night animals.
City hall's sign in red reads
Belfast Says No. In the bookstore,
four hefty rows of poetry.
We walk by the Opera House,
trimmed bright in green,
rebuilt quickly after the bomb.
You must feel the blood booming when I see
the first British army soldier, his automatic rifle
held tight as a baby across his chest,
or when we cross the stop point
where the law pulls a car hood up, searching.
Daughter, children with ruddy cheeks race past us,
giggling soft. In an alleyway, barbed wire wraps
around a pipeline. At the Crown Pub, we eat
ham and cheese sandwiches and sip a Guinness.
Outside Queens University, I buy band-aids
and purple socks for blisters, lean over
to pull them on. Military tanks drive past.
Two Royal Irish Regimentals with boy scowls
and machine guns point toward the sidewalks
of people. The pedestrians ignore them.
When I get home, I'm cramping and fear miscarriage
like the last time. The next morning,
news reports one bomb went off last night,
another scare this morning. Belfast people
live with this. Daughter, you
will see my risks like an insider,
unlike your brother.

You'll catch the way soldiers point
the machine gun right at us.
And the delight I find in blackberry crumble
and cream we eat in the coffee shop
over the streets with Mozart blasting
through the pipes.

Gémozac, France

Weighted under water. The eastern Atlantic pulls down. Sing
the *chant de mort*. Every night, hear crickets in the lime tree
outside the window. • You thought you knew: ancestors with
throats cut, dragged behind horses, mothers hung upside down
in front of babies and told, *Renounce*. • Something always burns
in you; this is not a horrible thing. • Fall in love with farm
France's low clouds, with cognac and wine, with grapevine and
barley in June. • Mother wrote: *Protestants in France--the new
king cut your ancestors' throats, all written in a memoir by his
great grandson*. You thought you knew. • The word *knew,* so
boring. Tiring. • Low fields just out of Chartres headed south
soothe and blanket, *calme*. Want only to sleep. • Hate Paris,
just for a moment, as ancestors loathed it. Like farmers hate
Paris, as the peasants before the revolution wanted to spit on
the king. • Love every crumbling wall here, each *maison* taken
over by doves, each vine in the field and all rainy weather for
good crops. • Remember your ancestor, riding at full speed
on horseback to this town. • In a rental car, startle his equine
ancestors, grazing in fields. • Embrace those descended from
denouncers, torturers, killers. • It's in my blood, *sang, lignage,
énergie*. • Forget. Remember. • Rise up and love this place,
once under water. Dig your hands in until you reach blood, mix
it with air, dirt, water. • Sunflowers will bloom outrageous in
August.

Barley

—Gémozac, France

Out of limestone and peasant heartache,
barley pushes up—stalky, stubborn,
gold aristocrat—with help from the sun.

So charmed by this place the wheat caresses
even the ruined *maisons* and all rubble fallen
around them. Their flowering heads determine

their way towards Cezanne skies, trusting
to the rain. These grasses burn with life,
like the smell of bread rising at a *pas*

cadence, releasing the fruit of cereal,
of whiskey and beer. Their stalks dance
on the *Arc de Triomphe*, while the tortures

of the world fade into granite's back story.
Clustered close here, even tractor tires only
bend and do not break this fierce miracle.

Dovecote Cottage
—*Gemozac, France*

When I left home, summer had laid down its
hot dusty body, unbuttoned its pj's sighing,

as wind rustled the dusty green. I was reluctant
as a worker on Monday, heavy as religion.

But now I'm an open French road with my
mother in low farm country where a sunset

is orange cashmere in the cool late spring.
Our ancestor, a protestant, fled by horseback

through these fields during religious wars.
How the world's priorities shift like these

low clouds dappling the grazing horse's back.
Like a tardy love between mother and daughter,

surprising as raspberries in the garden
beside the Dovecote cottage where we stay.

A stone wall beyond sets cozy limits—
inside lavender is budding, outside, endless

squares of gold barley. This late spring month
pronounced zhwah(n). *Take this,* my mother

says, a command to pleasure, handing me
a garden treasure. It tastes of carrot and earth.

The late sun, a joy raining light mist in us.

iii. red bridge of the forever river

Hanoi Waters Pantoum

The Red River no longer runs with blood,
And Cindy says men in Asia are criers.
Its people are drunk with rivers and hills.
A vet said, We killed our own dangerous druggies.

Cindy says men in Asia are criers
And Allen wept with vets in Singapore.
The Red River bridge was bombed every day.
A white pagoda floats in Koan Kien Lake.

Allen mourned with Singapore's other war soldiers.
Yet Vietnam's rains bring banana flowers.
Banana flower salad, white pagoda.
The Vietnamese have 100 words for happiness.

I try for happy, the long river sliding south.
Vietnam's rains bring banana flowers.
Vietnamese determine to be happy.
They smile like in no other country.

I try for happy confusion, watching lakeside Tai Chi.
At night, lights are lamp wick and loom, silk blankets.
Some nights the lights blink out.
Vietnamese women sew silk garments flowing like water.

At night I picture women sewing silk blankets in lamplight,
Drunken with rivers and hills.
Vietnamese sew silk garments that flow like water.
The Red River no longer runs with blood.

Ode to Turquoise in Vietnam

Praise whatever washed blue into green,
sleek as a barracuda sliding through Borneo's

waters, a color that cannot be emptied,
that sounds like a harp but it made of bamboo,

is the one hundred ways to say happiness,
the color and slap-clatter of my daughter's flip-flops

as she floods the floor with ballet in an ex-pat bar
to the tunes of *Abbey Road*; a bar that smells

of the sweat of vets, the color of shorts worn
by the toddler straddling a moto-bike with his dad;

it is the taste of lime and cocoanut juice,
the breathing of moonlight and cliff-sea love

and lotus. Chinese lantern, it echoes light
like bells, pierces the bellies of clouds,

absorbs the shirts of women gossiping outside
the silk store. It swishes in the Aussie girl's skirt

as she wanders down the street, is
answered by the lights on the cell phone

held by the Vietnamese boy behind me,
is the color of my embroidered silk purse,

is what the mermaid is married to.
It waters the red hot heart, blankets

the homeless child, is the calm beyond war,
will offer itself to the too warm earth.

Red Chaos: Old Hanoi, June, 105 degrees

Monsoon slaps the cab window,
  and we whine our way out of
    floating street lanterns and garbage.

Lychee fruit reminds me of rickshaws,
  parasols and stray dogs humping.
    It's okay to hate a place. My teen

daughter sipped wine, a pickled
  cobra trapped inside the gigantic
    jar. In Jade City, a man said

to her, *You have very pretty eye.*
  Unless you're the Dalai Lama,
    you'll be swallowed in the black,

sealess night of contradictions here.
  Temples? We pass one—urine baked,
    soaked, baked again—and glide on

to the hotel. Our taxi driver says,
  One day a year in China, everyone
    must kill ten flies that day. Shock

has its limits, I'm learning. Pagoda
  song of a city—even the kids
    begging can scheme in this scam.

I *could* stop the cab, shell out my
  wallet to one scavenger, change
    her life. How do you make peace?

Pho Bo, mister? a street vendor
        shouts as we stop at the hotel.
                Her rotting teeth slice my brain

into melon pieces. The sidewalk
        is a shallow pool for surfing
                through the legless. Behind my own

back, I'm dancing in my red chaos
        shoes for this Pagoda song of a city,
                                for this crazy place.

Sacraments of Rice
—Ta Phin Village, Vietnam

It throws straw for raincoats, hats and shoes.
It hardens like water buffalo horns.
Its fields, bright green lakes.
Its shape, the slit of cobra pupil.
Oh, blood and body of cobra and water buffalo.

I don't want to choose between white and brown, hulled or saffron.
I don't want to think Chinese, Japanese or Korean.
I want you to walk with me between the plush grasses,
      cross the red bridge of the Forever River,
        and see the Hill Tribe people bending.
I want you to stand on the red bridge listening to water, damselflies
hovering,
        far from porcelain plates and fine flatware.
I want you to smell the ox and fowl.
I want you to fill your hands and bellies with earth's cool pearls.

To My Daughter at 12 in Vietnam

When I die, there's nothing
that would save me like
that night you cried into my lap
over the Hill Tribe girls—

We'd traveled ten hours north
on old trains from Hanoi
into steep green mountains,
and met girls your age

who'd never seen a plane or
lived with running water.
They are so poor, you said,
they have nothing. But
they still give you things.

I stroked your hair and let
the Vietnamese karaoke
from the bar across the alley
drink in our room. That night,

you fell asleep to light rain
on your face. In the morning,
I asked you if lightning struck
your dreams. In your half-waking

eyes, as if I were still the world,
you wrapped me in your arms.

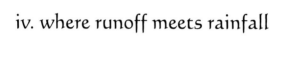

iv. where runoff meets rainfall

Coming Home

When a mother leaves, a child
thinks she has died. So when
I arrive after two away weeks,

I first hear Ariel chattering
Or is that cawing,
yes, cawing

like jay birds, her brother and
father mute in her blue house.
They all stand on the white

porch as I arrive and parade
down the steps. "Hi, Mommy,"
Ariel says, as if I'd been

to the grocery store. Then
without pause, I have come
alive for her, and she walks as

if to her own wedding with her-
self towards me, arms out like
kite tails and she is inside

my chest of bones and blood,
holding. The birds chirp
around us. Dylan and Michael

stand back like soldiers and
she rests her head on my bony
shoulder as if it were

a permanent pillow, as if I had
rolled away my own stone and
this miracle of found

lostness is all there is.

To My Children on Father's Day
At Wakulla Springs, Florida

We walk the gash of road pressing
magnolia leaves dead and crisp with our feet
into summer dirt smelling rich and rank
of forest as we float to the boat ride attraction.

On board, over water, the echo of human voices
tremors across the current, smell of charcoal
orbiting us in perpetual late afternoon.
Father's Day to Father's Day

I am always your mother.
This scenery, centuries old,
penetrates you both;
I have curled into this landscape

for 40 years, watching as everything
around it seemed to oil, sink,
slide into cement. Do you see
this miracle: a springhead that pumps

400,000 gallons of water per minute
into the river, nine miles down to the gulf?
On the cruise, we drift past
wood ducks, anhingas and moorhens.

The boat's tourists gasp at mullet jumping,
chant in unison their song-of-awe spotting alligators.
Sabal palms scrape the top of the boat as
dragonflies mate in midair.

The pickerel weed purples;
cypress trees feather their leaves.
Apple snails lay eggs on bulrushes.
My son, my daughter, we will all die

someday, but not now, not now. Look—
black egret and green heron, yellow-crowned
night heron babies—exotics for me, even.
And resurrection fern, cabbage palm, swamp rose,

O, the yellow-breasted warbler!

Planetarium Field Trip

Sitting beside my teenage son
in the dark, I am dizzied by things
like a moving night sky
the idea that Jupiter has thirteen moons
that a tornado has been zinging
the planet for the past 400 years
that the sun has been exploding for five billion years
and my son has gotten to the age
where I can no longer touch him
in public. Dizzied by things like
that Martian sand shines red, and
we live on a rock
that floats around in space,
that I started my mense cycle today
and can't concentrate on
the sonar or canyons, crescents, buttes of Mars
and that earlier my four-year-old
daughter refused to wear a nice dress
to school, but mix-matched for a rainbow effect
getting instead the bag lady look,
that the planets whirl round and round
the sun in an expanding spiral
wheeling around.
I float and spin and grow nauseous.
The star light above fades as lights come back on.
I look at my sandy-haired, black-eyed boy
in the midst of his awe, his growing.
We are run by rhythms
we cannot see,
not the five o'clock traffic,

but the sun's coming and going,
the gravity of our lives.
The north star, Orion, Cassiopeia,
the moving waters of our planet.

Planets

One day daughters stood in their mothers'
kitchens wearing the red of Jupiter. We said it:

I might get married, but I'm *never*
having children. Other mothers orbited

nearest us in a sky dry as parchment.
We were direct as bullets, or scattershot

as the twenty-one-year-olds we'd become,
wristwatches set for star-billions of years.

We toured in the silence of our mothers'
tragedies, stewed in our own star collapse,

smug children gone lazy. As if we could pull
back gravity, blast black holes. We needed

music that hurt. Our later years kneaded us
towards our riper pulps, so we pushed our mothers back

into us—sunlight, gasses, plants, animals,
water. Ocean spirits round with the tide.

By then we begged the Fates to make
clown planets of us, yes, mothers.

Blessings
—for Donna Decker

Dylan skip-runs ahead of
me and the baby, down
the rut road chasing his own

space of air to the mailbox.
His eight-year-old pockets bulge
with remnants of rocks, bird nest, throat-

tightening ache of absence, his natural
father. His ashy knees knob clean-boned
and coltish as he disappears

beyond the woods into the saffron
meadow, then back onto russet clay road.
Sun breaks on my daughter's

back as my son heads back, this tottery
protective man dance of his, hands full—
big brown box of my Swedish coffee

under one arm, a wild nosegay of
white and red field flowers
in the other fist. For me. Dark

boy, moon flower. His eyes look
to me steady brown as tree bark.
Quiet as December stars.

He drops the rest, hands me a gift
that came for Ariel. Pink wrapping paper
peeks out from brown mailing

wrapper—printed hearts, bears,
balloons and the inscription,
"Baby girls are a blessing."

My Baby's Hair Is Dirt

black and rich as we walk the carpet
of pine floor towards the straight
clay road to get the mail
I take my baby right down
As if life was a straight line

Her chest on mine a brassy meadow
lane, her brow tastes salt lick
sweet, she googah's like the brook
that used to breeze beside the road
I take my baby right down

Past blackberry blossoms white
as the moons rising under her nails
and vines like her veins that stand
close to the skin as yellow moths hover
As if life was a straight line

Almost there, she hears the highway
ocean howl, cars so fast
her eyes startle big and round
as the earth at the monster
I take my baby right down

To the plastic newspaper box a nest
spins perfect spiral in the way her hair
grows out, berries beside blood red and
dangerous as what got her here
I take my baby right down
As if life was a straight line.

Pushing

At almost two, Ariel pushes me in the porch
swing, pushing a blabbing baby question the way
I *bla-bla* to her, like squawking mockingbirds

in our woods, asking: *Do you like to swing high?*
Does the wind feel good? The swing crow-squawks,
she jabbers answers. When she pushes me,

I fall hard for my daughter, here in piney woods,
her eyes tiger-stripe black, skin like milk, chiclet
teeth, hair earth brown. Mothering me like I imagine

my mother did. This could be any movie of
mothers falling for their daughters all over the world.
I hold my arms out to her. She spies thirst there,

ache, and she shakes her head: *No No No*. Day lilies
poise like daughters, burning ginger, *No No No*,
                              she says
                                        dodging shadows.

Stars on the Sand-spit

Dylan and I wade in the lowest tide,
spot sea cucumbers, fiddler crabs,
tiny mussels. He picks up driftwood
clustered like stars with barnacles.

Don't take that, it's alive, I say. In
mud, we nearly miss the starfish
slathering on its stomach, and stop
to watch its belly dance. Lifted

curling legs, a hundred tentacles
wavering at once. How like a hand
a head, two arms and legs. Who
knows--did space tug at ocean

so long it made its own stars?
Stars now tingle under my skin,
my son and I walking on water
before tide pushes back over

this secret life we've found.
We wheel about the stars, back
and forth, starfish and ocean moving
slow and sure as bloodless sun sets,

stealthier than human eyes. I've
bought these gems stiff-still in
fluorescent tourist shops. Planets
circle as we walk to shore,

our hands empty, arms full of star shadow.

They Showed Me the Creek

my son says, pointing to his arm-gash,
grease-colored and long as bacon, so

we walk down the rain-smelling tar road
to see this place past sweet gums, black-

eyed Susans, the jewelweed and Madonna
statues in yards where the house plan is

duplicate multiplied by duplicate, to the lower
place, moist, shady woods and a steep cliff

smelling swampy, crammed with maidenfern,
licorice fern, spiked lobelia and common

blue violets. Where tree frogs sing their
bellies out. We lean into the fifteen-foot

drop of landslid water, where runoff
meets rainfall, creek, trashy ditch,

whatever it all is. My son shows me
the stomp print of his foot, where he tried,

son of a bitch! and nearly fell in, nearly
breaking I-don't-wanna-know-what,

holding on by his own arm to luck
and life and an oak tree trunk. Blue

tail skinks, a lightning-struck slash
out of pine trunk, the chucked stereo tuner

half-buried in the water's gunky floor.
Even in the suburbs, nature is not

a negotiator. I put my arms around
my almost teen boy, the safe evening

burning down, the air ionized, frogs
chorusing the swamp, licking

the evening clean one more time.

Small Vespers and High Waves

The gulf is elephant gray today
stampeding a storm from the glass
door of the motel onto sand. Radical

waves as Ariel sleeps, bronze and
milk mixed baby. Michael drinks wine
red as communion, quiet as TV static,

sound off, our glances beyond words or
bumpy horizon paling, purpling, and we
rest after the storm. I want to call the name

of my daughter's eyes: not bluegreen,
not graybrown, but saffron rings around
the irises as if the sun waits behind them.

Then she cries rising like her yeasty
breath between us, her utterances a
pulling like the tide. We turn to waves.

Daughter,

When I die, throw my ashes into those late
Lavender Ironweeds, the sun-craving black-eyed Susans,
     The Crimson Clover and horsemint, into the native
Wild flowers of Florida, showy White Indigo, the white-

Flowered red-fruited Partridge Berry.
I want to come back hardy as a boxer, old as Indians,
     I want to be sipped
By the stiff-winged buckeye butterfly, the Gulf Fritillary,

Tiger Swallowtail, Painted Lady.
Burn me down, cut me clear, and watch
     My seeds spread and return, surprising everyone
With a torch of yellow abundance, of inch-long, three-

Budded purple blooms, of Resurrection Fern.
Let the floods come and the droughts. I'll be dry one
     Year and muddy, then you'll see me along the
Highway, orange-yellow bursts returning year after

Year. Think of it: my grandmother splitting open
Into bean-red flowers now that she's shed poverty,
     A father's beatings, drink, her last
Breath. See her in the pink Purple coneflowers, spread-

ing butterflies' darling. And my Cherokee great-
Great grandmother no longer giving birth, dying young
     Before seeing seven surviving children grown,
Blossom, as she now into creamy white wild

Horehound or the easy re-seeder Red Sage, attracting
Hummingbirds and my day angels, sturdy Sulphurs.

My daughter, pick me by the hundreds in a meadow
And plunk me in a jelly jar on your table, or

Watch me lean into the grasses. Learn to stretch past
All mothers' terror, love me and the more
That is me, as the Cherokee knew to love
What is underground, the earthworms and the moles.

Fear of Drowning, Mother's Day
—*with gratitude to Sharon Edwards Ryals*

Suddenly you evaporated. Your
girlfriend and your sister in the pool
naïve as sea lions, said you'd wanted
to paddle out on the inner tube
so far you couldn't see land.

Your family gathered on the third floor
beach house with binoculars, but like
plankton, you were invisible. Mad
Captain Bly, your grandfather called
Marine Patrol. I clutched at my sister-in-law

as if she were a buoy. My clothing felt
darker than widow's black. This
mother fear, worse than my own
drowning. Surf thundered like
vomited tears, and I thought of sharks,

of exhaustion, of breathing water.
Seaweed drifted onto shore, black
like a lost inner tube. The phone rang.
They'd found you, thirsty, dazed, caught
in outgoing tide, and pulled you in.

We drove like clumsy beached
fish to the cut where they brought you
back. Your eyes shone like black pearls,
hair ropy seaweed mats. You've seen what
Neptune can do. This time, he gave you back.

The Bear

At eleven my daughter wavers between
everything, today wandering our house
in the woods singing *lai lai lai, lailailai-*
lailailai, waiting for the bear to knock at

the door. Birds sound their super-soprano,
flitting by pines in a china blue day. Down
hill, the watershed pulls and is pulled. My
grown son grows dreadlocks, twirling twigs

of a cardinal bird's nest, and today stops
by to plant blueberry bushes. He bicycles to
work in the dark because cars ruin the planet,
he says. TV is tuned to Oprah where parents

have lost their daughter to a car wreck.
A man by accident killed his wife, yet
another shot his son thinking him a robber.
And yesterday my Alaska friend said bears

will soon be extinct--ice caps melting. I woke
last night with a ticket for careless driving
near bicyclists, for overheating the sky with
poison. Tonight I sing *lai lai lai, lailailai-*

lailailai as my husband hunts the refrigerator
for tomatoes, cutting as I sauté, pouring broth
and beans to simmer the soup we all will eat,
celebrating the cool season upon us as we wait

for the bear who may or may not knock at our door.

v. field that cups a pond

Before a Summer Thunderstorm

The world is mostly water,
you think as you walk outside
headed for the car with a cup
of coffee and a list of errands.
The lightning flashes, rumble
of thunder takes four counts to
reach you, but the trees do
a rumba in air. No one will pay
you to stop, to watch, to imagine
a time before motor boats and
submarines. You sit anyway,
arms wrapped around your knees.
Forget grass stains on your pants;
this wind could take you and
break you like plastic toys.
Where did we get the idea that
we have control of anything?
The leaves seem to dance like
seaweed under water. We are
bottom feeders in the forests,
slow, small, and have insatiable
fire instincts. Maybe the lids
of our eyes are surfaces
of water. When we sleep, we see
the deep, roam the stars. You
realize time is passing, your errands
waiting, coffee cooling. If we slow
down enough, will time reverse?
You pick up your coffee and head
to the car. Above, leaves make their
music. The water above glows hot.

Ode to Driving at Night

You've seen them, too, from the bus,
a car, on a evening stroll when the moon
hooks its quarter self into a black sky. Glimpses
in on homes you'll never know.

On the highway, you see them in amber windows,
people shadows so close to your speeding car
their blur startles you. Even closer sometimes,
they hang around on bare bulb porches

leaning into one another. Then it's dark again.
More lights in windows flash by like summer
lightning. The mystery of others—buzz of refrigerator,
sigh of the dog after it turns and settles on the rug,

how the house creaks and settles at night.
Do they, like you, remember the angle of daylight
shining through the house, do they come home
tired, swollen and relieved. Do they shift

their children, soft and heavy on their laps,
and does the smell of garlic linger after dinner?
You've driven all day under the too blue sky,
rocks breaking against the wheels past remote country,

and you pine for your own crowd of family,
your car slashing through the stretch of asphalt
into the black; the last of their lights humming
a polished copper gleam in the window behind.

Swallowtail

It's a passion, joining words, all these forms of English,
here where I happen to rocket along the road,
clinging to particulars, dense and living:

the sun blinking its disco ball through live oaks
that yawn and stretch limbs across the road.
On the radio, a linguist says *ill* means

great to rappers, and *the tangle of
Spanish moss* is a phrase that steers us
away from *me,* uncombs its gray,

daring to touch down on us as we burn
past in our speed. Around a curve, lime
green clover clutches towards light, climbing

a red clay bank. *Pro nasty* means *the best,*
the linguist says. I slow, pull off, stop before
a grassing field that cups a pond. Like paintings

on Japanese tea cups, old pines swing above
the water. Horses graze, swishing tails like
limp wristed girls. I've always yearned

to stop here, and haven't. Am I *so* busy?
In the south, the linguist says, it's *y'all,*
up north, *youse,* sometimes *yern.* We cling

to our quirks of English, the linguist says,
as the world changes faster than cars whisper
past in gusts. Overhead, a swallowtail kite

screams. How *ill*! *Pro nasty*! Such grace
in flight. The word *endangered* takes too
long, feels too clumsy to stop it all. And how

did we
end up
too busy
to watch?

Charleston Garden

This is the city slamming
its Sunday noise through the streets,
the soot and grease smell like any New York,
just past the shortest day of the year.

This is me walking beyond it and atop
the Battery wall where the sun butters
the Ashley River below, Charleston's oldest
houses across the street. Suddenly the breeze is like fruit.

This is me neither missing my family
500 miles away, nor my job,
40 hours a week away,
and why think of that now?

This is the world today, French,
studied, graceful and lavender. Or maybe
this is just me, alone,
and we all need a rest.

This is the arched and glassless window
to the gate enclosed by tall walls
of the Greek Revival home across the brick street,
this is its flash of green and me lured into it—

A garden—sabal palm and four columns.
This is coveting: a venial sin.
and who could resist marble birds, wrought iron
chairs, the Greek urn, Georgian frieze,

even a cocker spaniel asleep?
This is our lives, civilized and wild, neither;

we can't make up our minds, so build gardens.
This is Eve. Now, she loved her garden,

but she had to leave.
This is the deepening sky standing over me,
this is restlessness, me with or without family.

And this is the grape arbor pulling slant light
through the piazza.
This is my family in my garden;
I will bring them here,

but not now.
The sky is low and lavender.

Ode to Jasmine

There's so much to relish on this earth,
despite the inconveniences of our weather--
take the ill-named *Confederate Jasmine*

that builds its leafy clouds on the windblown
trellis along the driveway, petals wicked
white, plush aroma of sandalwood and orange.

Even in this drought, as white magnolias
dissolve to mustard shades, the jasmine's
swaggering stems reach like the limbs of

a woman towards sky, its lacquer-leaves
the green of black jade. And it's not a bit fussy—
no belled skirts, no wilting--plant that bleeds

the color of thick milk when cut. Heavy and
light as the feathered underbelly of a cat,
I've seen these jasmine marquee breezeways,

emblazon brick walls, even lace a chain
link fence. Pinwheel of a flower, bittersweet
reminder of our transitory nature, it jostles

with bushy life upward in our stumbling world.

September Air

O months of blooming green heat,
the rain we so needed and now
wind like ice water glittering,

hickory nuts dropping down on
the tin roof, the sky a reflection
of the wounded, how jaws of ocean

and whirling roar have eaten
our favorite city whole. The drowned
shores' thousands, the sorry buses

for refugees, lunacy of looters'
dreams, of salted waders and
dull ocean bloating trees. What do

we know of real trouble here?
Now we see that salt water buoys
bodies--how can we now walk

on water? All's quiet--the saxophones
leak now. I remember midnight city
swimming, the tropical red face of a

fortune teller, the Voodoo Museum
with its love potions, brown curtain
of the Mississippi breezing below

the ferry, even as refugees,
without knowing, go to Idaho, Utah,
to the seaweed ashes of Kansas. These

escapees believe in a ghost wind,
how it flip flops dust or mud,
Oz-like, a field of illusions. Let

us be moored by elements. Wind,
scatter seeds to hold this earth.

The Sound of Drought

Take a sprinkler whispering its fire across air, the fast
clack of cicadas drumming out their belly song.

Add the clink of glass murmuring wine between friends;
cricket rubbing its wing song. Chime of your mother's

long distance laugh. Measure out the hush of leaves,
linen scratch of lizards shuffling pine straw, a sigh of night.

Capture the pop of jasmine shooting the air; ripple of
earth's one big breath in, and low clouds rattling dust.

Place these in a bowl you call your hands. Lower your face
into them to listen to your fears sloshing thirst.

Baptize midday with history's ears. Listen
to the ocean for days after dry days when the purr

of raindrops tears the sky, roaring wet-meets-
earth smell, crows afterwards awe-aweing.

Broken Chimney in the Surf

Because the ocean is a fence,
because the broken chimney grows
      velvet over brick under the surf
because our door step takes in exiles
because wind shear singed our homes
      we shiver on cool porches ringed in rain
but the sky is bone-china, blue and January
not a month of hurricane teeth.

Because a net is a fence
because we brick the sand
      by the velvet surf
because fish flop on our door step
because we are singing the rain that rings
      our homes, we shiver in this gamble of burn
but the sky is bone-china, blue and January
not a month of hurricane teeth.

Because there is no fence
because the ocean darkens in our growing
      chimney smokestacks and melting velvet
because we exile the deep sea doorstep
because our homes dissolve the sea creatures
      the rain rings acid
but the sky is bone, china, blue and
January is not a month of hurricane teeth.

Because a fence cannot ride an ocean
because we can build no house when our bricks
      keep getting stolen
because we are exiles on the doorstep
because we thieve the shells off sea life

we shiver until our rickety porches rain heat
but the sky is bone-china, blue and January
not a month of hurricane teeth.

What I'll Tell the Martians
—for Mia

I'll tell them of our handshake, a greeting,
our tick tocking clocks, how we measure

to scare ourselves into fearful and tidy
ideas, like the number of babies who die

before five. I'll take them to the Georgia rain
forest of trillium where fairies live, even if

we don't believe, and show them how water
is where we gather, how the sound of

summer crickets in the evening can bring
on ecstasy. I'll explain our cigarette and

nun habits, point out camels and *djellaba-*
wearing women who drive motorcycles.

I'll admit to our obsession with hamsters
wheeling in cages, and to my mean tiny

heart. I'll have them swim in the Wakulla
spring that pumps out a hundred thousand

gallons of water every minute, and they
will shiver with cold, so I will take them

to the south of Asia and let them touch
the hot stones of the temples. I'll show

them the dry rooms where we argue, *Is
poetry dead? Is the book dying? On what*

else can we meditate to desiccate? I will
explain Amazonian fishes big as pigs. I'll

show them Saharan refugees stumbling and
staggering, skin stretched over their skulls,

faces frozen in death grins. Martians can
watch the auctions where paintings sell

for millions, they can hear wars that cost
billions, I will slap them silly when I feel

like it, because I'm an American, I can. I
will offer them *café con leche* from Spain,

ask them to smell cumin and cardamom, to
touch their tongues to fire of Mexican *mole*,

to listen to the clink of Swarovrski chandeliers
 in Prague, the turquoise silk of Vietnam, I'll

take them to a room, scoop up all the sadness,
all the dead, and put them in a blanket in

that room and show wars' grief over nothing
important, nothing, and close that door.

They will hear robins, jay birds, the half-
growl-half-purr of grackles. I will show them

my infant niece covered in blisters from
a disease that won't let her skin stick.

I will ask them to take hands with me,
float into a circle and pray for earth.

vi. swim uncaught

Ghazal for Writing Students

The least of my worries is my students.
I say these words to myself daily, my students.

Tonight, they read at a dark green bar. My students
know how every day is a Tragic God,

They smoke cigarettes, the most shy of my students
turn up beers and shout with my students.

Some of them are not my students
yet. They read to Allen Ginsberg that they, too, my students,

have seen the best minds of their generations, my students',
destroyed by madness, starving hysterical naked.

Leaning into the microphone, one of my students
writes that her father told her "boys will be boys." My student

says she kept part of herself deaf. My students
clap and cheer. They listen to the story about the boy who

relishes wrinkled apricots offered by a dying woman. My students
sit at odd angles almost touching the shoulders of my students.

They laugh at the story about the storyteller who put no sex
in his story. "It must be a failure," he says. My students

laugh at Hollywood, my students
sway over the poem about razors, how close we come, Students,

to the bone each day. My students
know every day chases them like a Tragic God, my students

feel Comic Dog pant and drool at Tragic God's heels. My students,
the least of my worries, my students.

The College Teachers Job Hunt
—Modern Language Association conference, 1993

Heavy and whole-boned, we feel like the seven cows
sitting sculpted between the skyscraping buildings
of Toronto. We've spent a month's salary for

suits, motels, we've flown from Florida to Canada to find
jobs in the U.S. Frozen Lake Ontario aches my
southern blood. We septuplets stand black-suited

in line, but without a conference badge, I'm not
allowed in. *Meat Market, Cattle Call*, I bellow,
thinking horse snort, scent of hay, sweet feed taste.

We are the dark milk of the market. At the glassed-in
Westin, all I want is bare feet and horse sweat mingling
with mine. Is a bridle like a job? *These cows are so*

cool, Kim and Tom say. My prince will ride up and
present me with a cow soon. *Cause I'm cool and
you're no*t. The hairless cows of this late capital

culture are tomorrow's ground meat. Eating a burger,
Tom says, *Take, eat, this is my body*. We bleed out
in laughter. The cows slump on stony grass. We want

to touch the sculpted beauties downstairs in the cold.
They will heal us from greed. *¡La corrida de torros!*
these cows shout. The sound scrapes and echoes the sky.

Leaving Kansas

and the cottonwoods, forty-below winters,
dry wind raking corn and wheat stalks,
the limestone-mangled and unfarmable dirt

did not make me want to look back.
To cow dung, cow blood burned on Fridays,
cow muscle, cowboys, dog food plant stench

and small-town, no theatre'd tyranny.
No ambiguity, no ambivalence here.
I floored it to Florida, my fifth generation

home, to hoses hissing a snake song,
to the yeast of green, stopsign red
of cardinals, the growing time of tomatoes,

midsummer's evenings, scuppernongs
ripening on the vine and clay red as
our human rust. I choose heavy

rain, who knows how many words
for water, live oaks drooping drowsy smoke
of Spanish moss like brazen, lazy sin.

The honeysuckle gone, blackberries already
eaten, magnolias wilted on their trees,
but not me, not me, a wildflower brought

by an underground river of desire, miraculous
revival of Ophelia, back to moldy bathrooms
and mosquito bites, to lizards, yes, even roaches.

Nope, no apologies for snakes, melted butter,
sweltering noons, spoiled milk, burnt skin,
spider webs spun, I take it all, home.

Alligators and Academic Careers

Gusting and puddles for two days
as lights rim twinkling ivy that clings
to a colonial brick downtown. Folks
raise glasses of Merlot indoors.
My bayou bones say *Where are your
        bare feet, girl?*

I'm daring to dream sand dunes with
drifts like origami. I wanted this career,
and now it's dread, reading my story—
what must this faculty think of the alligator
wrestling Everglades Indian story?
        Who are they, who choose me or not?

I begin to smell myself--hank of
mildew, vaporous place that grew
me, its umbilical fierceness of wild
grapevines twisting under live oaks
and snake flesh. This Virginia town,
        foliage pruned into elegance, indoor

flowers blooming opulent, yes, civilized.
Charming. If offered this, I will say
Yes. Something hurts my throat, aches
the belly. Outside the hotel room, I walk
the balance--steep weeds and treacherous
        ditch, a border I balance across near joy, next to

regret, following forgetfulness. My accent
is all wrong--I've been twanging the gulf
when I talk. Cherry trees will bloom here

soon. Cherries. Blackberrying swampy woods.
Watch for snakes, my mother said. The older gods
       wait, grow, belly slide, and swim *uncaught.*

Students Return from Spring Break

Their backs were sticky caterpillar before,
my now-winged students, but they're lolling

in. I do not even recognize them, coming
from the brackish water between cheap rough

motel sheets and stomachs roiling with
soured rum, not having given much thought

to how ocean is azure or why we sleep
to the sound of waves rolling in like barrels.

Has the memory of this assignment due today
hit them like the shovel in the face? We come

to order in the College of Business Fidelity
Union Classroom. But no--they're not lolling--

they're all military attention, eyes beaming
darkly. I feel the prickle of caterpillar hairs

itching the back of my neck. *Dr. MJ,* they say,
Your neck! My eyes open and I see shimmer

colors of their wings. They play their impassioned
parts fiercely, they parody TV talk shows,

poke fun at Paris Hilton, laugh at their own
cowboy bawdiness, translate teacherese

into their own language. They get that the world has
no meaning except the one they themselves find, and

still these students flap those blue-black and orange
and buckeyed wings. *Viva la vie, viva la vie*, they say,

their smarting performances batting me with
powdery wings in the color of flight.

vii. the blood-black swamp

Live Oak

In the dense moss, branch fungus,
the smell of deep woods, you
sang out in blue tears when
the buzz sawed the live oak

down and I was young and thin
and arrogant as an arrow—
A live oak? Crying
for a *live oak?* I glowered, but

the resin had seeped into
my blood and I withdrew,
terrified of your flower and thorn
knowing, your honest moment,

Mother, you scissored at
the silence of despairing trees,
you were a sudden mouth
torn and talking and,

and yes it touched me,
the leaves, the lives, the honey-
suckle all became one in me—
I can't tell hips from tree limbs so

how could I not go on
remembering you, your mother,
my daughter, in our torrential
green, in the natal woods,

as long as I draw breath.

Horse Grace

Once Cathy, Susan and I searched
for the missing pinto, Maude, in the woods.
We found her fallen against a tree broken
with her weight. The maggots swirled in
and out of her mouth,
her ribcage still heaving in,
exploding out air.
We bolted from that life in death,
hid our heads under pillows as
Cathy's mother pointed the shotgun
to Maude's head. One day, my sister
Barbie's Tennessee Walker, Lady, reared
from some invisible fear by the pond,
galloped her through branches and brambles.
At each bound where the horse's legs
rose off the ground together,
Barbie said she could feel
the lightness of her death.
briars that gouged skin, the hurtling,
her face hitting hard clay and after,
nothing, until the ambulance. Then that day
the blood ran down my thighs, rusty,
not skint-knee red. I told no one.
At ten, I knew only that this was me
and my horse. And what we all came to was
abandoning their oaty sweat, mossy
muzzles, the gamefree kiss on the forehead.

Confluence

We limboed under the *CLOSED* museum
sign to sit at the confluence of two rivers,
all of us wanting to steal stars, breathe
brackish water and sear words onto paper.

Sand gnats bit our eyes' edges, but still
we six sang Christmas carols, floating
ghosts, a gathering of meshed intimacy.
We yearned for anything, each other,

everything, flamenco feet, echoes of jazz
down the hallways of our houses. Security
is shallow, we thought, and in a way we
were right, reckless, lusting for crossed

currents. Drunk as greedy gods, we ricocheted
rocks, careened into the mangrove opaque,
baring our essential selves, peeing
together. The moon slid up from naked

trees. I lay alone on hard rocks, nauseous,
(insecurity is deep but not still in the stomach),
the two rivers sloshing together beyond,
a shipwreck. I wanted to throw away overflow,

and in the distance I heard their *Silent night,*
Holy night. The stars laughed, pulled me back,
held my hair as I puked, said, like my mother,
Don't take it all so seriously. In the wind,

did I hear, *Just take it, this life, it's yours.*

Remembering Pop

Evenings came down graceful as a cat stalking
that summer Pop and I sang
"Swing low, sweet chariot."
He pushed me in a homemade swing
under oaks and crickets and a moss
Florida town. My grandmother
and mother would call us
home. But time was drenching us,
its gardenia scent cloaking us
as we'd pass its petals
later on our walk around the block.
We swung hands
like father and daughter
in dreamy moonlight,
the streetlight.
We threw palm nuts
into pearly Lake Lancaster
and watched the rings
go from wedding band round to
much larger than ourselves.
He let me shred the paper tree to pulp
in the cool dusk
before we headed home.
My mother told me years later
that the family knew
he had cancer.
So did he, losing himself
from early morning
to night in the bourbon, she said.
But what I remember is
singing, "Coming for to carry me home,"

our voices flashing
like mackerel,
him swinging me out
into that brown sky.

Mary Elks, 1904
—remembering what Great Grandmama told me

They've taken my dolls,
packed them away,
given me teacups
and white sheets instead.
Fifteen is old enough,
Mama had said.
My chestnut braids
were so long Eugene Smiley dipped them
in his inkwell
at school two years ago.
Now they're twisted
into two tight circles
against my head.
I've put on the white chiffon dress
and said, "I do"
in the wooden church
beside the graveyard
covered with live oaks and moss.
Now I'm waving good-bye,
horse and buggy squeaking
as we pass the blood-black swamp.
The faces of my family
have turned moony.
Mary Elks, I secretly say.
Mama schooled me in this:
the man next to me,
my husband, I must always
call "Mr. Ryals."
He stands a food-and-a-half
taller than I,
hawk-nosed from his Cherokee mama,

handsome for an old man
of thirty-five.
Mary Elks, I say in my head.
The dress I changed into
is tightening, tightening
around my waist.
Mary Elks, I say,
You don't even know this man.
I look back, catching the last glimpse
of my family,
their bodies like down
mattress feathers floating
skyward in the August heat.

My Cousin's Wedding
—Atkinson, North Carolina

This *must* be a Jane Austen novel,
my uncles both ministers, and
we *are* gathered, as they say,

in an 18th century rural charm
church. You know the tongue-in-
groove wood, the stained glass. Thank

God (so to speak) no Jesus-on-
the-cross. Orchids center these pastel
windows. You can run your hands through

crushed velveteen pew cushions like
cat fur. Comfortable boredom, Presbyterian
communion, wafers and grape juice,

no exoticism, but a sense of ceremony
present. Speaking of exotic, my beautiful
youngest cousin, "the wild one," they say,

like me, married twice before, a butterfly
tattoo on her arm, a five-year-old son.
The groom is a Christian karate black belt

with a prematurely silver ponytail.
I like him. *This* marriage will work.
He's got a job. Hear the family taking

a collective southern sigh of relief. My uncle,
father of the bride and family orator, marries
them, reminding us: *clothe yourselves*

with compassion, kindness, patience, forgiving
each other. My intellectual friends might roll their eyes
to heaven (what heaven?), might scoff, might mull

logical argument, like this tortured head does,
so I brush the velveteen cushions the color of wine,
hankering for a sip of anything red. Meanwhile,

center rear, my daughter and her cousin, both
thirteen, dream of their own big day (or maybe
the boys at the hotel pool back in town, or maybe

simply, with Presbyterian ennui, the lyrics
of the Pussycat Dolls song, *Don't you wish your*
girlfriend was hot like me?) The groom's sister-

in-law weeps. The noisiest young cousin stage
whispers, *SSSHHH, WE'RE IN CHURCH!*
to the quietest cousin. The war in the Middle

East feels planets away from this, the blueberry
capitol of the world. *The earth is the Lord's and*
all that is in it, I read from Psalms, and though this

family could conduct a hot, spit-worded debate
on the meaning of "The Lord" or of owner-
ship and gender, who needs more dickering? And these

words make me just now inexplicably happy.
Happy as a dog with its pack, or as
Elizabeth and Darcy after saying their vows.

viii. tide at its neap extremes

Camping Out in Front of *Suspicion*

You trail after me home following
the party, where we talk about
playing games like Scruples,
and I want a cigarette bad, but
I don't smoke, and four times
you talk about sprinting out
the back door but
at five a.m. you've slid off
the sofa onto the floor
and I say *Let's camp out*
and watch Hitchcock, so cover
you with a blue-daisied sleeping
bag, a yellow blanket with crisp
brown leaves *From a real campout,*
you say, while I make a bed beside.
The VCR hums its lullaby, and
we slumber like virgins, not touching
breaths. You dream I collect men in cases
and smoke them as I dream
someone stands among daisies
yanking their stemmy necks.
It's not till morning after you've
gone that I think of lips on feet,
stomach to stomach, teeth
at the neck and hands around things
that I feel sweet heat aching
like a suspect.

The Kiss

This morning I watched cardinals and towhees
light on the window feeder you gave me
at Christmas. I called to thank you

for these moments; they come fuller
and more briefly these days. The sky
is leached, leaden, sinister looking or

delightful, removed as a mystery
novel, either way. I was looking at *The Kiss*
by Picasso, woman's eyes akimbo,

man's nostrils huge. I don't know,
I don't really want that. Or Rodin's
The Kiss, the guy so muscular,

she with pointy breasts—no. But if asked
to paint or sculpt the world of kiss, I'd decline.
On the phone, I read you a bad line

from a student story; you tell how
your students got the multiple choice
problem backwards. We laugh at our lines

and backward guesses, and say goodbye. Then
you call right back, say *I love you* and
You're beautiful. I ditto. It's romantic ruse,

the beautiful part. Still. The birds have gone off,
gathered at the bare plum tree above the fountain.
I wonder how they kiss.

Waiting It Out

Call us Woodsmoke and Sweetgrass.
Help me picture this: dropped off
onto a rutted road, in the middle
of blood. Ours. Say that I'm losing
fetal blood, that we wind up in ER.
Say the cramping could mean death.
Suppose we drive home, wait. Maybe
we think of her Sweetsmoke, him
Woodgrass, our baby dancing with
foxes, fishing the river, or imagine
vertebra, heart, brain breaking apart,
trailing out, a forced removal. We don't
speak of these things. Can you
picture it? We walk the canopy
of dirt road, smitten by honeysuckle
fragrance, trill of invisible bird,
pine needle floor blanketing the woods,
the mourning dove. We sit inside
under Grandmother Sun, trying for
purification. We bicker, helpless,
our love like clean water. What
gives life or snakes it away?
Tension burns like cedar smoke,
scent rising in air like prayers.

Blood

My husband is a river of legs in our bed.
The blood of my hope beats through
his arteries, his calves, down the slight

swell of his ankles, up to the musk of
his chest, beating inside our eyes.
Whose blood is this, loves we never knew

and long dead? Did we know one another's
capillaries in other lives; the owls ask *who*
who who-whoo in the woods out the screen

door. The breeze brings in night-blooming jasmine.
Should I raise my voice in psalm or song
to calves to jasmine and breeze? I found

what part blood takes in love, in daily
slumber, in gratitude when his blood clotted
at his leg. It was Spring, squeezing my heart to panic.

Every day now we whisper night-blooming
and breathy loveyou's, secret breeze between
us, awareness of legs of feet of blood, sending

itself like a river bed back around back around.

In the Motel Room

The day after I miscarry
we drive to my west coast, the Emerald Coast,
find a cheap room for the night
where sand feels fine as confectioners
sugar and squeaks under our feet.
You don't want to talk about it, you say.
The wind whisks your glass-broken voice
away the way a bird scoops up fish and
disappears. I guess I can't talk either.
We walk barefoot back to the room.
I slump like a walrus onto the mattress and
watch you search like always in these
small rooms. New rooms. Homes-for-the-night.
You slide open drawers.

Look. In this drawer, our daughter's eyes gleam
green as yours. In the next, her laugh
contagious as you claim mine is.
She would have been born my sign, fire sign.
You shut that drawer with a decided slam.
Three times today on the road
you said you still want children.
The change of tides, constant as rhythm.
You even think I'll slip blood through your fingers.
You search the room like a child would.
Kitchenette cabinets, drawers, tiny doors.
Where are your children? Look. In the closet.
Our daughter stands tall as your mother
in her dancing tights, poised and waiting.
You shut the door and whirl around.

Look! You say, an alarm clock by the bed!
How lucky can we be? We sure got our money's worth,
you say. And we laugh, we laugh, trying
to bring her back to us.

The Sestina of an Unmarried Mother

You're looking for a husband, he says
perched on a stool watching your work
at feeding your pregnancy's hunger.
It's his cutthroat kidding you hate,
the delicious pain of possibility you love.
You would not keep just anyone's fetus. Need?

No. Want. This ham and cheese sandwich you need
but not his summer sleepy eyes that say
in an evergreen way I love
you or Why are you so damn angry? Your work
is his—rejections, revisions, a hatred
for imperfect story, obsession with language, hunger

for the sound of ocean, of bodies cresting. Hunger
with need. You don't want need, fear need.
Can he know how a pregnant woman might hate
to reply No to marriage? To say
yes can mean death even as a tiny life works
to feed itself on both your loves.

Sometimes you lust for his voice, his love
faulty, musical, lazy, hungering
to fill up a juice glass. He's seeped into this work.
What is it that a woman needs—
or wants like old Freud would say.
You get so sick of grocery dailiness, hate

paying bills, buying the hated
car part when what you'd love
is to buy silk clothes that say
see this bulge, body some women hunger

after, at times, even think they need.
They don't know how it hinders or helps work.

You long for him like work.
His long legs, his laughter. Hate
your empty space, lonely bed and broken need.
When he taunts you about a husband, love
his boyish hands under his chin bringing back hunger
that flares into an answer you cannot say.

Love Poem for Michael from Northern Ireland

I'm no good scouring for love words, even pregnant,
even pregnant again. A steep drop from the Poets' House

past the burrow, the cows, to the foggy Irish Sea,
Scottish Hebrides a blur in the distance, you

in America. I've searched for words in the late
grape summer sky, the same night-indigo

as the lobelia by the door. I want to say—what?
Barry walks the half mile up Islandmagee's road

to the pay phone, through pastures of sleeping
sheep under midnight quarter moon. Simply,

he must call *Sile*. He found words—her lap and hair
make his nest. I've used up *I-am-yours* words long

before you. Paula tells us Estonians means poets,
ancient word for liars. I know what I can't say.

At Queens College in Belfast I see Declan again,
sculpted Shelley face, haunting, how he's your

North Irish twin, red-haired, dressed in black,
while you dress Florida surfer blue. Janice reads

Plath's *Blackberrying,* and daisies spread from the vase
wide as hands outstretched. Poised before playing

your jazz piano, the hands I want on my stretched
belly skin. Rod says we become one, not one,

says love is a business of heart-in-the-throat. I miss
your dirty tennis shoes and sunglasses, the musk

of your stomach, legs propped up on the sofa,
book splayed on your chest. I know you—you'll

say this isn't about you. But I know everything living
here breathes a green belly breath that never forgets you.

Postcard for Michael from Spain

Primavera, spring, soaks itself in
azul sky. *El sol* gilds everything
through unseasonable cool, serene, busy.

I wish you could be here now
to visit Neptune and the seven goddesses with me
at the *Plaza de la Virgen.* In the morning,

our necks are washed with sun's warmth, feet cool
in Mediterranean breeze as businesses screech open
their metal doors, *el tiempo* full of promise.

Purple petals from the tree above litter
the red brick plaza. Last night
I dreamed of you, reached for you,

gave you *besos en el cuello* on a Spanish tile floor.
We dove into the fountain, the moon
a stone whose light transported us,

our skin fragile and resilient as the skin
of pudding. What have we known about
traveling until now? You're not here.

Meanwhile, I tend the flock of students,
loud and big as bullfrogs, eager as birds
for bread. Inside the cool of cathedral

rushes me. High above, the sun
burns through the stained glass window
below the gothic ceiling, *uno, dos, tres*

rays of light pushing through
the fragrant heavy smoke of incense.
While others kneel and pray, the church bell

tolls eleven, and I wait for the gold red burn
of summer, of aquamarine beaches,
of hot sand. I watch across the sea,

las montañas, the desert, for your reflection.

Love Poem, Fall

This week filled October's moon with obligation
and the first holiday near, we've grown distant and
biting with each other, my husband and I, for days,
slowly disappointed, feeling covered up like

wood on our deck by leaves brown and dry with
busyness and duty, and what's required just to go on.
And so this Friday just before Hallows Eve, our daughter
with friends all trick-or-treating in pajamas, our son

working on his monkey-style kung fu, we pry
ourselves away, drinking wine and eating scallops
at the restaurant on the bay, slumbering
in our parents' house by the gulf. As a child, I spent

weeks discovering how long I could float in salt
water, like it was some dehydration race, amazed at how
fingertips pucker like a grandmother's enduring mouth.
Like this was some secret journey of endurance or abiding.

Tonight, the moon, slightly past full, the autumn gulf
tide softening our urbanized lives, we sleep
hard, love hard early the next morning to the sounds of
cardinals, blue jays, wrens in pines whispering outside.

Rising from dreams, we take our coffee on the deck,
and my husband tells me to look out front—the lantana
he worried would never grow, now a bonfire of orange
flowering shrub, at least a hundred tiger-stripped butterflies

treading beach breeze, sipping nectar. We stand, coffee mugs
in our hands, watching the wind symphony in orange,
the fall finally pulling itself through too-warm air,
a ghost-shawl of celebration resting on our shoulders.

How to Make a Baby

Live on an island where wind
brushes the palms, where
you cannot walk without
seeing the glisten glance off
water, where no one but
the tourists lock doors.
It will help you believe.
Find a man. He must have eyes
that stun you with their mirrored
oceans, with knowing too much.
You think he is beautiful as sand.
Watch him. He loves to sit
on the porch at the white wooden
house where dolphins roll beyond
the back yard. Notice that
children gather around him
the way sandpipers are drawn
to a morning shore. Go
ahead. Tell him. You want a baby.
Nothing surprises him.
You begin to pay all attention to
sky and water, air and fire. Soon
you can distinguish grackle from crow,
heron from egret, know you have
lived as a bird before. Make love
as if you are moon and he is tide
at its neap extremes. Read
Shakespeare and Milton. Find Ariel.
Look it up. In Hebrew it means
Spirit. Read ancient Celtic poetry
by women. Find Dylan. Look it
up. In Gaelic, Son of the Sea. At

the midnight lapping, call them
to you. Their spirits enter.
These are ancient. They will
teach you with salt and blood
what you have needed to know.

ix. skimming like lost history

The Importance of Columbus' Discovery of America:
On Fire Mama and Water Boy 500 Years Later

Fire Mama wears black-and-blue American jeans, shiny black boots to stomp the fire, she drinks rose-blue firewater, leaps round flames on blood velvet nights.

Fire Mama breaks open at late afternoon bliss, her time; Water Boy, all water, paints in aquas and burnt oranges. He's pale, has blue love for Fire Mama and cynic wit. She has no *wiowah,* husband, likes it that way.

Water Boy jumps on all the beds with Fire Mama, they smell heart pine wood the bedroom walls, ceilings, oak floors. Fire Mama, Cherokee name Fire Starter.

Fire Mama and Water Boy yearn to sleep in every morning—school's okay but takes up so much time.

Fire Mama and Water Boy live on pasta, butter and milk, can't pay electric bills, listen to music in minor keys or Rap. They pick up pine cones in the woods to paint instead of cutting down a tree for Xmas.

Fire Mama buys candles for her blue writing horse, her tangerines or raspberries in a bowl, buys paints to mix-and-match for Water Boy. Grey-brown feathers spread around her house like bouquets. Chaac, Mayan god of sun, hangs on all her walls, she collects Timucuan pottery, reads Cherokee lore to Water Boy.

On foggy Blue Monday, she stops in to hear the singers at a towny bar. Thin, blue-skinned-and-haired, Fire Mama likes her shape feathery.

Fire Mama can't sleep winter nights, even if she's partied, sometimes wants a man in her bed. She could indigo dance by the moon fire.

Water Boy loves to stay up all night, too, though blonde, he's thin, tall, dark-eyed intense, beautiful as Amonsoquath, the Bear.

Fire Mama throws big parties and sometimes takes downers, curls up with sweetwater Water Boy by the bonfire in a sleeping bag, sleep so like cocoa as the party roars around them.

Fire Mama wants snow and beach and 42nd street and swimsuits at the same time. Her Water Boy does, too, is a Mexican Island smelling flames and eucalyptus.

Imagine this, Fire Mama says, swinging on the front porch with Water Boy. *Aliens—from another planet—show up and say 'HEY! RENT'S DUE! PAY UP OR GET OUT!! AND BY THE WAY, YOU HAVEN'T BEEN TREATING YOUR FURNITURE SO GOOD, EITHER, SO YOU DON'T GET YOUR DEPOSIT BACK,'* she says. *Half of the renters bite the bullet somewhere between here and there. It's called the Trail of Tears.*

Water Boy remembers dinosaurs, draws Dracula with bat tattoos, boa constrictors spilling out of its ear, horns on its head. Fire Mama laughs like water. Water Boy sees nothing funny about it yet, but that's not his job. Fire howls in gales, water, when it gets big enough, runs in gurgles.

They walk the dirt road looking for fox tracks, for cool rocks, for pecans, for weeds with cottony seeds they can blow up in the east in a dry hope day.

A Word to Sylvia Plath after Seeing
Heptonstall Cemetery

How such beauty lives in Ted Hughes' country, where
    steel towns' blackened brownstone buildings stand. How
    huge they stand, as if unashamed, across from green
    moors, grass and sheep grazing.

How the Calder River still bubbles and rolls past
    sycamores and ash, under railroads, through towns, how
    during the Industrial Revolution the average age of
    death on these moors was nineteen.

How we drive up the hill onto cobblestone streets,
    to a forgotten village on the Penines, how
    the wind slams into the moors off the Atlantic.

How I am shivering from the inside out in mid-
    summer and put on a sweatshirt, how
    we all step over stone grave tops to get to the grey church
    in this grey place.

How we find out incidentally from the lay
    minister, that Ted buried you in the Hughes family
    cemetery behind this church. How
    your body was not taken back to America.

How you hated it here in the Hebdons, and the
    people hated you, how
    he knew that.

How the lay minister says you're a bit troublesome
    up here, buried quickly, quietly, and how

the townspeople below don't much like it—a suicide buried
on sacred ground.

How Ted has written your name black on the stone,
how feminists from all over the world vandalize the
H-U-G-H-E-S off the granite.

How he exhumes the stone, has H-U-G-H-E-S replaced in black,
to shove the stone back into unsettled earth, how
this has happened over and over since your death.

How achingly gorgeous this cemetery as we walk
through tall oat grasses, the wind blasting the hilltop
over white crosses that seem to float atop the graves.

How some graves are covered in orange poppies,
others blanketed in purple pansies, still others spread
with hot pink foxgloves.

How your newly-hughed grave stands unkempt,
only a thorny pale rose bush cut back,
so severe it stabs at me like this wind in my ears.

Eve Explains Herself Years Later Outside the Garden

What was I supposed to do?
I got so damn bored in that
avocado and pomegranate
garden where we ate and
ate and never felt full,
could smell no cedar, saffron
or sweet gasoline. And had
no knowledge of a stinging
nettle, tooth of a shark, the
speed of automobile on the
highway, the colors of a
coral snake or even the weepy
feel of rain. And where god
was a man—I got *that* message.

And Adam busy being perfectly
happy, scheming with that tick-
fat opportunist god of his. I
heard them scamming each other.
God told him crap about how he
molded my breasts from Adam's
rib. Adam reassuring god that
he was the only one, ho hum.

What I wanted was a woman
to share eyeliner with and talk
about why fruit rots. Children
to play Ninja versus the dino
with. I wanted to slide my hand
down Adam's backbone built
from chance. Have a beer and

a smoke. Just hear one song
 by The Bangles—*I'm going down
to Liverpool to do nothing for
the rest of my life.*

A Broken Sestina

How could you keep your head
in this cathedral? When you grow
up Protestant, kneeling is drama,

like Lot's wife turning to salt
when her biblical city burned,
their world changed. Forever

changed, like ours, soldiers be-
headed before our television eyes.
But the world never changes,

the way wars are lost, always,
and rock us, finally to kneel.
The nuns kneel now, black-and-

white headed after they quit
sunshine at evening time,
the moon a rock in the seared

sky. This sky running blood orange
red, away from our control. *Light
the world with candles of change,*

burn incense and kneel, the priest
would say. The stone above him is
carved with two sculpted men, each

grasping a cut-off head, the prey
held high. The priest hopes Mary
and Fatima will change the way

the world works. Not so in this too-
full world where prayer becomes
prey, becomes head, becomes

torture, then beheading. Can we
stop, find a way, pray, knell. Hell,
kneel for our world to change.

The Fisherman's Widow
—Cedar Key, Florida

What circles the house just beyond my view,
calling to my bones. What to the west,

where the gulf lies. Sunset, the farthest beauty,
and lamplight on the hall table, echo of life

that rings yellow about the house.
Luna moths hovering the screen door.

I am an ocean of sadness, the whole world
an ocean broken only by the promise

of islands, losing ground, the shadows
on my robe seeping deeper. From midnight

the hours drag like low tides, then again
swallow the shore. A small octopus dives

deeper, searching the fading face
of my husband, picking at the secret lock

of his undoing. It will take years for the reefs
to love him, to understand his name, to dissolve

him to memory and to repeat it to the vast
sky. Hungry wind through hot screens,

moths clinging. Banana spider grips
the corners of the porch, her black and yellow

striped legs long. Her amber belly spotted black
and white and bulging, my sole namesake.

Laundry

—Corneglia, Cinque Terre, Italy

A woman hangs afternoon laundry
on a balcony so near mine we could
touch. Below, the Mediterranean's
clear bottom slips its snaky suit from
soda bottle green to Donatello's blues.

Her towels bob and back-and-forth,
riding wind tide. She does not see me,
her hands a frugal grace littered with
socks, her thoughts crowded with
dusty floors. Far away, mercury clouds

leak a river into the sea as the sun turns
to fire behind it. Where is the mountain
tip the Cyclops heaved into the sea as
Ulysses taunted him? The greaves and
helmets of wars, long rusted, have closed

under water. Can I hear the fifty sisters
ride seahorses on surf? Clean cotton bouquets
the air. This woman next to me, face hard,
queenly—server of the house, the waiter,
the grieving war wives of centuries lining

her face. But today, the chaos of house crashes
into the fact of magic. Cliffs lift straight up—
the waves sound like tricky women laughing.
To remember that passion flower blooms across
the hill, I want to live long. The goats whelp,

as goats did when Ulysses slaughtered them wild.
Thank you or *There's time enough to dwell in dust,*
I suddenly want to say to this woman. Tonight, my friends
will revel in fragrant wine. We will suck juice of anchovies
between our teeth as windows turn fire orange.

Sailing the Mediterranean

The clouds are the backs of lizards
in this *Rockaby baby* blue blanket of
childhood dreams. How could I get so

lucky, here where the Phoenicians cruised,
where these waters grow olives, grapes,
and oranges *in the tree tops*. There's the moon!

That half cookie, sly and disappearing over
time, like the names of this ocean—
The White Sea, The Middle Sea, Our Sea.

When the wind blows, I am dizzied by
movement of water and Zephyr wind, the Sahara
Sirocco that can blister throats. Let this buoyancy stay.

Those cranes on shore at the port, like
my brother's toys, orange blue, yellow—
they want to touch sky! But the semis remind me

of the semi that ran over my car thirty years ago.
The cradle will fall if I let it. *And down will
come baby*. But I am not Ulysses without charts,

I'm loaded with luck and Lorca's moon winking,
to hell with fear mongering, a *cradle*.
I am as alive as shepherds of the she-wolf

who birthed Rome, rank as wet sea fur, the sun
pouring nickel onto this chop and soup of salty lake
and sunken stories, and on the boat, the whoosh, skimming

like lost history of
        Europe, Asia, Africa,
                and all.

About Mary Jane Ryals

Author of nonfiction, poetry, and short stories; editor at the *Apalachee Review* literary magazine; and research associate at Florida State University's College of Business, Mary Jane Ryals has added a new title to her portfolio: 2008-2010 Big Bend Poet Laureate.

She is also the 2006 winner of the Second Annual Yellow Jacket Press Chapbook Contest for Florida Poets for her work *Music in Arabic*. Her short story collection, *A Messy Job I Never Did See a Girl Do*, is available from Livingston Press, and her nonfiction book, *Getting into the Intercultural Groove: Intercultural Communication for Everyone*, was released in 2006 from Kendall/Hunt Publishing Company. Ryals holds a Ph.D. in English from Florida State University.

The Moving Waters is her first book-length poetry collection.